Mats Sundin

Mats Sundin
The Centre of Attention

Scott Morrison and Lance Hornby

Copyright © 2000 by Sun Media Corporation

All rights reserved. No part of this work covered by the copyrights hereon may be reproduced or used in any form or by any means—graphic, electronic or mechanical, including photocopying, recording, taping or information storage and retrieval systems—without the prior written permission of the publisher, or in the case of photocopying or other reprographic copying, a license from the Canadian Copyright Licensing Agency.

Canadian Cataloguing in Publication Data available on request

The publisher gratefully acknowledges the support of the Canada Council for the Arts and the Ontario Arts Council for its publishing program.

We acknowledge the financial support of the Government of Canada through the Book Publishing Industry Development Program (BPIDP) for our publishing activities.

Key Porter Books gratefully acknowledges the following sources for permission to reproduce photographs:

Sun Media Corporation:
Dennis Miles, 10,12,16,45,63
Michael Peake, 11,37,44
Mark O'Neill, 18,24,25,66,67
Greg Reekie, 20,21
Craig Robertson, 23,37,52,73,80,89,92
Kevin Kerr, 25
Warren Toda, 26,80
Jack Boland, 40
Fred Thornhill, 62
Mike Casesse, 48,49,64,83,84,85
Zoron Bosicevic, 65
Trish Hickey, 76
Stan Behal, 50, 46, 51
CP Photo Archive:
Kevin Frayer, 15,19
Ryan Remiorz, 25
Chuck Stoody, 30
Moe Doiron, 57,58
Frank Gunn 66,72
Reuters:
Andy Mettler, 17,32
Gary Meshorn, 81
Bruce Bennett Studios
Bruce Bennett, 36,39,42,42

Key Porter Books Limited
70 The Esplanade
Toronto, Ontario
Canada M5E 1R2

www.keyporter.com

Editor: Glen Williams
Photo Research: Jillian Goddard
Design: Peter Maher

Printed and bound in Canada

00 01 02 03 04 05   6 5 4 3 2 1

Contents

Introduction 6

1 Centre of Attention 10

2 Rising Star 26

3 The Draft 36

4 The Nordiques 38

5 The Trade 44

6 Life with the Leafs 62

7 Quest for the Cup 80

Introduction

I still remember the day Mats Sundin was traded to the Toronto Maple Leafs.

It was draft day in Hartford, back in June, 1994. And it wasn't so much that Sundin had become a Leaf that caught everyone by surprise, it was the fact that Wendel Clark was the major cost to acquire him. The deal made perfect sense, that if the Leafs were ever to get over the hump and win a Stanley Cup they needed a guy like Sundin, but it took people a long while to accept that trading the immensely popular Clark was still the right price.

The way Sundin conducted himself in the days that immediately followed the trade didn't make it any easier to accept, either. While Clark was all over Toronto, dabbing his eyes and accepting another toast and farewell salute, Sundin was nowhere to be found, hunkered off in the backwoods of Sweden. He was invisible . . . as invisible as he often made himself on the ice in the playoffs, some cynics suggested.

He dodged reporters who had flown from Toronto to track him down and when they did catch up to him, Sundin was less than enthused about the prospects of sharing his thoughts about becoming a Leaf. This from a guy who had, essentially, just been acquired for one of the most popular Leafs of all time. Buckle up, we all thought, this is going to be an interesting ride. And it has been, but for entirely different reasons.

Just as he has developed and improved on the ice during his time in Toronto, Sundin has also matured and grown off it. He has come more than just an outstanding hockey player, he has become a team leader and a guy who understands and happily accepts and meets the responsibilities he has to the public.

The growth of Sundin—the person and the player—was never more evident than last spring, in fact, when he helped lead the Leafs to within three victories of their first appearance in a Stanley Cup Final in 32 years.

Despite the occasional howls of dissatisfaction from the stands, despite airwaves sometimes crowded with criticisms between games, despite forests of trees torn down to print sometimes indifferent critiques of his efforts, when it was all said and done last

In the second round of the 1999 playoffs, Mats Sundin showed that he was willing to stand in front of the net and take the punishment often necessary to score playoff goals.

spring, Sundin stood front and centre in the Leafs dressing room to answer for his team's performance. And make no mistake, it had become his team.

That is called growth—as a player, and as a man. Indeed, for a guy who seemed to have the weight of the hockey world heaped on his shoulders last spring, Sundin felt he grew an inch or two during the playoff experience.

There's little doubt that he seemed to get stronger as the post-season progressed, finishing with a team-high 16 points in 17 games. He had moments of greatness against the Philadelphia Flyers. He got better and meaner against the Pittsburgh Penguins and ultimately outplayed Jaromir Jagr. He had eight points in five games against the Buffalo Sabres, despite the tough checking and the Leafs internal meltdown.

There was little doubt that Sundin, who was the most second-guessed and under-appreciated Leaf all playoffs, was also a major reason why they got as far as they did. He was a big reason why a franchise that had been floundering for a few years once again found hope and a belief that there may just be a bright future.

In many ways, the Leafs and Sundin emerged as one. For the first time in his career, Sundin, who had never gotten beyond the first round of the playoffs, experienced the joy of playing in May and playing rather well. And through it all, he was there day after day, wearing the captain's 'C' on his chest and answering for his team.

"I got more experience in those 17 games than in my previous eight years in the league," Sundin recalled. "Everything came together . . . You realize this is what you play for."

Thinking back about that conversation and thinking farther back to the day Sundin was first traded to the Leafs, it's as if they were dealt two different players, and in some respects that's the case.

Now, it's still unclear how history will remember Mats Sundin the Maple Leaf. He has carved out a rather distinguished career for himself to date, but his is still very much a work in progress.

It's also a work that seems to be getting better with age and maybe, just maybe, for Leafs fans starving for a championship, the best is yet to come. With his renewed sense of focus there's a sense when you talk with Sundin that anything short of a Stanley Cup victory would not justify his trade to Toronto. Afterall, we know that's how a lot of the fans feel about him—and have felt about him—since the day he was traded to the Leafs.

SCOTT MORRISON

1 Centre of Attention

Sundin was on holiday in northern Sweden when he learned of the trade that would bring him to Toronto.

The rugged Torne Lappmark, a four-hour drive north of the Arctic Circle, is where Swedes go to get lost.

For a harried Mats Sundin, in late June of 1994, this was the ultimate deke. He'd slipped out of Stockholm with brothers Patrik and Per and two cousins on a fishing/hiking excursion, far away from the media on both sides of the Atlantic that were following his contract squabble with the Quebec Nordiques.

But on this trip the solitude was not to last, nor would tranquillity come easy again. Sundin's rising star was on a collision course with the centre of the hockey universe.

First came the sharp chirping of a cell phone that informed Sundin he'd been traded to the Toronto Maple Leafs, going from the Siberia of the National Hockey League to its hub city, in a bold six-player deal for the Leafs' beloved captain, Wendel Clark.

Though he expected a trade somewhere, Sundin quickly realized the price of clearing up the contract and joining a contender was leaving his friends in Quebec for a certain degree of vilification in Toronto. He did not relish being a foreign interloper who usurped the meat 'n' potatoes Clark. As the 23-year-old Sundin digested his new lot in life—and the trade bulletin elbowed Sweden's World Cup soccer team from the headlines—the family departed their main camp for some fly fishing, intending to get far away from the publicity maelstrom that was now sure to follow.

That is, until someone in the party detected the sound of whirring rotors.

"I'm standing there with my fishing rod, and out of nowhere this helicopter appeared and landed about 20 feet from me," Sundin recalled with a laugh. "It was a television crew coming to ask about the trade. I was absolutely shocked they'd come to the middle of nowhere. The cameraman must have come right from the city, because he was wearing a white t-shirt and in no time he was covered in bugs.

"Then another helicopter showed up, this one with a newspaper reporter and photographer. I was pretty mad, because we'd only told one person where we were going. They must have paid him off.

"But from what I heard later about what was going on in Toronto (where Leafs' president Cliff Fletcher was under attack for the deal), I was probably in the right place."

When Sundin stopped off the next day at ex-Leaf Borje Salming's hockey school in the mining town of Kiruna, the Toronto newspapers had joined the hunt, bringing him copies of their front pages that trumpeted the trade. Sundin nervously read comments from such influential voices as Don Cherry, who condemned the deal, and fan polls that ran about 60–40 against the trade.

Five years later, he's still very much in the spotlight that found him in the Arctic tundra.

Former Maple Leafs president Cliff Fletcher made the decision to send Wendel Clark, his most popular player, to Quebec in exchange for the young Swede, Sundin.

Borje Salming, the former Leafs star, shared his insights with Sundin when he was traded to Toronto and advised him to accept the captaincy if it was ever offered to him.

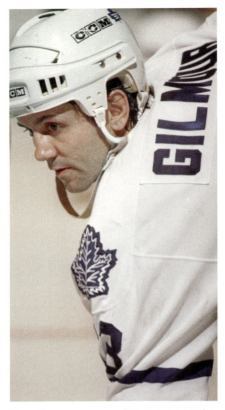

Sundin was named team captain in 1997 when the Leafs began their rebuilding process by trading Doug Gilmour to the New Jersey Devils.

Sundin led the Leafs past Jaromir Jagr and the Pittsburgh Penguins in the second round of the 1999 playoffs.

But now that there's a 'C' on his sweater, the skeptics are a minority and the Stanley Cup gets steadily closer for himself, his team and the hockey-mad market he now calls home.

"I came here as a 24-year-old, to a team filled with veterans such as Doug Gilmour and Dave Andreychuk," Sundin said. "I felt it wasn't my place (to be too vocal), even when I was alternate captain. Now, I'm one of the oldest guys on the team."

In June of 1999, after being eliminated by the Buffalo Sabres in the conference finals, no Leaf bore the pain of falling seven wins short of the Cup more than Sundin. But he refused the chance to hit back at the critics who thought he lacked the fortitude to take the Leafs that far.

"That's up to you guys," he said when asked if he'd silenced his detractors. "You are the ones who keep bringing it up."

Until the breakthrough of the '99 playoffs, Sundin had never been past the first round. Now the pressure is to go all the way in the new millennium.

"No one wants it more than Mats," good friend Tie Domi said.

"He and I have been here the longest now and he realizes he's not getting any younger. He's learned from other captains such as Wendel, Doug and Kirk (Muller). He knows it's his time."

From an assist in his first game as a Leaf on January, 20, 1995, Sundin has been climbing the club scoring ladder, at a 1.03-points-per-game pace. He's surpassed some of the great names he sees above him every night in the rafters of Maple Leaf Gardens and the Air Canada Centre and within two years should be in the top 10 scorers in the 82-year-old franchise's history. Only Darryl Sittler has won more consecutive club scoring titles than the six that Sundin is closing on.

Yet it wasn't until the grand old Gardens' closing on February, 13, 1999, that Sundin truly realized his link in the eight decades' chain of Leafs' lore.

At the conclusion of the ceremony, 89-year-old ex-captain Red Horner passed Sundin a huge Gardens' flag and in a strong voice said "Mats, take this flag to our new home, but always remember us." Surrounded by a few hundred alumni and an emotional crowd, Sundin had a visible lump in his throat. In a couple of months, he would help lead Toronto into its first conference championship in five years.

"To me, that playoff showed he had what it takes for the job," said Sittler, the former captain and Hall-Of-Famer. "The adversity he faced early in that (opening round series against the Flyers) with everyone on him for not scoring is one of the hardest things about being captain of the Leafs.

"I think Mats feels like he's part of the city now."

Sundin originally had doubts he was ready for the captaincy, which Sittler called "one of the greatest jobs in Canada." But there was no mystic meeting with the late King Clancy to show Sundin the way, no torch passing ceremony in the fashion of the Montreal Canadiens. The challenge was picked up far away from the Leafs' dressing room at an underwear factory in Stockholm in the summer of 1997.

"Borje Salming runs the company, and every year before I come back to North America, he gives me a box of underwear," Sundin said. "Doug Gilmour had been traded and there was talk I could be named captain.

"I said to Borje, 'if they ask, do you think I should accept?'"

Salming, who played a thousand games for the Leafs over two decades, didn't hesitate with his reply.

"He told me the Leafs once offered him the captaincy (in the mid-1980s) and he'd said 'no,'" Sundin said. "But he would have

On February 13, 1999, Sundin faced former Leaf captain Doug Gilmour during the ceremonial faceoff at the last NHL game to be played in historic Maple Leaf Gardens. Although Chicago won the game, it was a night to remember as decades of Maple Leaf alumni were celebrated on the same evening.

Opposite: During the closing ceremonies at Maple Leaf Gardens, Sundin and Red Horner shake hands as the Maple Leaf flag is passed on to be hung in its new home at the Air Canada Centre.

Coach Mike Murphy was fired and replaced by Pat Quinn after a disappointing season in 1997-98, Sundin's first year as captain.

taken it if ever given a second chance. As a Swedish (pioneer), it was one of his biggest regrets.

"He said it would be hard for me. The demand would be great from the fans, the team and the media, but I should never pass up such an opportunity."

But to this day, there's an anti-Sundin faction in Leafdom, who see him as too laid-back a player and undemonstrative as captain. They believe the Leafs' leader should be the eye of the storm, as Doug Gilmour had been when he almost single-handedly willed the Leafs into the 1993 Cup finals.

"I knew I had to be as good as I was before I got the 'C' and better afterwards," Sundin said. "You have to represent the organization and make what happens on the ice your first priority. A lot of the dressing room stuff falls into place."

Hockey Night In Canada's Harry Neale, the dean of colour commentators, has scrutinized almost every one of Sundin's games as a Leaf. If people think he's not working as hard as he can, Neale says it's just a matter of perspective.

"Mats reminds me of Frank Mahovlich or baseball's Joe DiMaggio," Neale said. "Those kinds of guys are so fluid and graceful that it looks like they're not giving you everything.

"Yeah, Mats is not belligerent, but there's a mile-long list of guys like that in hockey who've made it big. All I know is that I see Mats fight for the puck one-on-one and usually come up with it. You give him half a step on you, he's gone. He's got the best backhand in the league and he's the best in the league at cutting in off his wrong wing since Glenn Anderson."

Sundin not only had to deal with the Gilmour/Clark legacy when named the franchise's 16th captain, but a number of other issues on and off the ice. The Leafs missed the playoffs in '97–'98, as the conservative style that coach Mike Murphy was obliged to employ ran counter to Sundin's strengths. The roster upheaval that was sandwiched around the dismissal of Fletcher saw close friends such as Matt Martin moved out, while the losing, the Leafs' jokes, and a battery of cameras and microphones never subsided from September to spring.

"Mats grew unbelievably well into that job," said Bob Stellick, who worked with every Leafs' captain since Rick Vaive as the Leafs' former head of business operations and communications. "The biggest challenge to a Toronto captain is balance, but Mats somehow manages to leave all his problems at the rink.... Borje had turned down the captaincy and was no worse for it, so people wondered if Mats would be adversely affected."

Darryl Sittler presents the captain's sweater to Sundin. Sundin is the first European player to captain the Toronto Maple Leafs.

Fletcher was not among the doubters.

"I don't believe Sundin is the type of person you can yell at and scream at and wind him up," Fletcher said. "At the end of the night, Mats will have a point or two, and at the end of the season, he's your leading scorer."

Once primarily a scorer, Mats has greatly expanded his role since becoming captain. Although he still leads the team in scoring each year, he is much more aware of his defensive responsibilities and isn't afraid to use his size to reach the net offensively or to remove opposition players from in front of it.

On the Hot Seat

Sundin recognizes his role with the media and makes a point of showing up for locker room interviews win, lose or draw.

During his first four years with the Leafs, it mostly meant fielding a barrage of criticism about his play or the team's. Some players of lesser stature around the league are not accountable at all.

The Leafs six-week playoff run in 1999 saw major media markets from around North America and Europe work over the Leafs $7-million man, especially when he didn't play well.

"When it happens during a year like last year, it doesn't bother me at all," Sundin said. "I hope they blame everything on me, as long as the team is doing better. If we lose a game and somebody has to be criticized, I'm here."

2 Rising Star

Sundin visits with his father, a former goalie in Sweden, in the Maple Leafs dressing room.

Opposite: Sundin was a member of the Swedish National Team that won back to back World Championships in 1991 and 1992.

Tommy Sundin and Walter Gretzky had lots in common.

Both worked for National phone companies, both turned their homes into make-shift arenas and both were influential in their sons attaining National Hockey League stardom.

"It's amazing how my family did the same thing a lot of Canadians did—with the big hockey games in the driveway," Sundin said. "As kids, we dreamed about playing for the Leafs and the Canadiens.

"My whole family, including my mother (Gunilla, a nurse) are sports oriented—hockey, soccer, tennis, bandy—you name it."

The close-knit Sundin home was in a middle-class suburb a 10 minute drive from Stockholm, in what is today considered Sweden's Silicon Valley. Sundin's birthplace is listed as Bromma, but he was actually raised in nearby Sollentuna.

His earliest hockey memory was, as a five-year-old, hearing the fuss around the TV set when Salming received a standing ovation at the Gardens during a Canada Cup game against the Russians. Sundin was impressed for years afterwards that Toronto fans would think that highly of a Swede.

Tommy Sundin was a goaltender who once tried out for the national team. But he concentrated on a different career when he moved to Stockholm from a small town in the 1960s and eventually became a project engineer for the phone company. His work didn't stop him from getting out the pads and letting his three sons shoot to their hearts' content though.

Patrik, the eldest at 32, and Per, who is 24, were fair players as youngsters, but never got far from pick-up games. Mats, who began with a crude pair of skates by tying blades onto his boots, was also inspired by the growing Swedish invasion of the NHL and excelled at various hockey schools.

Not naïve about the chances of making it big in the sport, Sundin did well in high school and trained to be an electrician.

Even after signing a $22.8-million US deal with the Leafs in 1998, Sundin joked "I might need a career after hockey."

Young and able-bodied, he also faced a mandatory hitch in the Swedish army, where he would have done everything from peeling potatoes to firing automatic weapons. But that was on hold at age 17, when Sundin progressed quickly enough to crack the second division Nacka team, a farm club for Djurgarden in the Swedish Elite League.

That was his springboard to the national program, the honour of wearing the famous blue and gold of Tre Kronor. The lure of the NHL had no bearing on Sundin's desire to make his national team, and in 1989 he was able to play on both the junior national and world championship squads.

Years later, as captains of their respective NHL teams, Sundin, Ottawa's Daniel Alfredsson and the Islanders' Kenny Jonsson would credit the national program for helping them be better leaders.

Mats used the size he had added from off-season weight training to impose his will on opposing players during the 1996 World Cup of Hockey and the Nagano Olympics. It was widely agreed that he was one of the most dominant players in both international tournaments.

"One of the reasons we're likeable as captains is that the Swedish system puts the team first," Alfredsson said. "Yes, sometimes that's not always good, but we've learned a lot in North America and I think now you have a good mix."

Quebec's lack of playoff success in Sundin's early years had one advantage—it freed him up to play in the world championships. He had plenty of gas in the spring of 1991, going to Finland and scoring the gold medal game-winner against the Soviets. The next year, he returned to play a huge role in beating the Soviets and Finns for another gold, bringing him more national acclaim.

A bulked-up Sundin was also one of the most dominating players at the inaugural World Cup in 1996, winning the European pool with a highlight goal in a 5–2 win over the Finns. He faked Marko Kiprusoff in full stride in the slot and drew goalie Kari Takko

When the NHL switched the All-Star game to the North America versus the World format in 1998, Sundin got the opportunity to play with several of his teammates from the Swedish National Team. Above, he shares a moment with fellow Swedes Niklas Lidstrom of the Detroit Red Wings and Daniel Alfredsson of the Ottawa Senators.

far from the net for a backhand goal, a taste of the highlight goals to come.

"It's hard to understand how he did it," coach Kent Forsberg said. "Very few players can score a goal like that. Considering Mats' size, it's even more amazing he can be so mobile. He embarrassed the Finns."

Sundin used the added pounds to protect himself from being pushed off the puck, while at the same time enhancing his skating push from a standing position. When the World Cup playdowns moved to North America, Sundin continued to be a force, particularly with physical play that impressed Team Canada coach Glen Sather.

"That was the best game I've ever seen Sundin play," Sather said in the aftermath of a 3–2 double overtime win over the dogged Swedes. "He matched our guys hit for hit. You couldn't take him off the puck. He was the one guy they had who never wore down."

When Toronto missed the playoffs again in 1998 and Sweden failed to bring back an Olympic medal from Japan, Sundin took out his frustrations at the world championships. With future coach Pat Quinn watching from the Canadian side, Sundin had 11 points in 12 games pacing Sweden to the title. Swedes have followed his progress in North America with pride.

Leafs' sweaters in about 20 Stockholm sports stores were snatched up within a few days of the Quebec trade, and the baseball hat craze, fairly new to Scandinavia, has seen allegiance of lids split between the Leafs and Peter Forsberg's Avalanche.

The Leafs already receive good coverage in the Stockholm sports pages; their games are in demand on television, no matter if the live telecasts start at 1:30 a.m. Swedish time. Not a week goes by, home or road game for the Leafs, that a Swedish TV crew doesn't tail Sundin. He's quite accommodating, though he drew the line one day when a Swedish producer asked him to pose in the middle of a dangerous Bay Street intersection.

He is well respected at home for his charity efforts, which have included organizing a game in aid of old friend Rojer Andersson. A third-division Swedish player, Andersson ended up in a wheelchair after being hit from behind in a game during the '93–'94 season. Before joining the Leafs for the first time, Sundin brought together a group of NHL stars including Forsberg, Thomas Steen and Johan Garpenlov to play a club select team.

"I think he's the best loved player in Sweden now," said Gunnar Nordstrom, one of that country's top hockey writers. "He's been around a bit longer than Peter Forsberg, he's popular with fans and he hasn't lost touch with his home."

But like his Viking ancestors, Sundin would not cross the Atlantic without some hardships.

Mats-a-Mania Grips Sweden

Sundin has probably caused his share of lost productivity among Swedish workers, who've stayed up late through the years to watch his live NHL or international games on TV. Though Sundin and Colorado's Peter Forsberg are friends (Peter's father Kent coached Sundin on the national team), there is a rivalry between the big city Sundin and Forsberg's more humble roots in the small northern hockey factory of Ornskoldsvik.

In '96–'97, when they briefly dueled for the NHL scoring title, Stockholm papers created a daily story and chart updating the race between the "Super Swedes." When ballots were made available in Sweden for the 1997 NHL all-star game, the newspaper *Aftonbladet* urged countrymen to stuff the ballot box and jam the Internet to ensure one or both made the starting lineup.

Following: Sundin demonstrates his famous backhand as he flips the puck past Team USA goaltender Mike Richter at the 1996 World Cup of Hockey.

3 The Draft

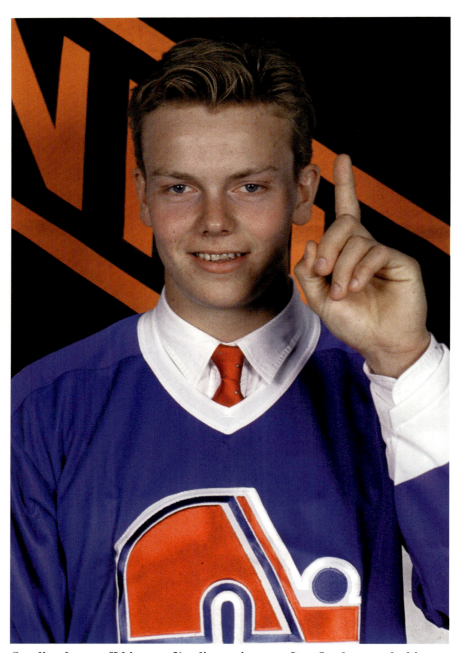

Sundin shows off his new Nordiques jersey after Quebec made him the first overall pick in the 1989 NHL entry draft. Sundin was the first European player to be selected first overall in NHL draft history.

The lanky kid that one scout dubbed The Swedish Beliveau was still unknown in the days prior to the 1989 draft in Minneapolis. Sundin had only 18 points in his first 25 regular season games with Nacka, which paled in comparison to 56-goal winger Dave Chyzowski, the top North American.

Sundin hadn't made the Swedish national junior team, which further obscured him from North Americans. But the Nordiques, led by chief scout Pierre Gauthier, had a presence in the Swedish League and were well aware of Sundin's electric finish in the second half of the schedule. The Nords drooled at his size and figured he'd grow another inch.

"If you saw him dominate in Sweden, you knew he would be a success in the NHL," said former Nordiques' coach Pierre Page, now a scout with the Minnesota Wild. "I'll bet you Mats was just 6-foot-3 (190 cm), 178 pounds (81 kg) when he first came to us in Quebec. Now he's taller and about 225 pounds (102 kg)."

By the time Sundin and his Boston-based agent Mark Perrone arrived in Minnesota,

Quebec's intention to draft Sundin had leaked out. Risking the first pick overall on a whim was a theme that played heavy in the Quebec media in the hours leading up to draft day, but with the tact that would mark his years as Leafs' captain, a polite and quietly confident Sundin won over both the team and the reporters as draft day approached.

With the announcement of his name, Sundin became the first European taken No. 1 in the draft. Watching from their front row table were the Leafs, who were only a point better than Quebec and the New York Islanders. After the Islanders picked Chyzowski, Toronto took Scott Thornton as part of an ultimately fruitless experiment of taking three first-rounders from the same Belleville Bulls junior team.

History, of course, would rule in favour of the Nordiques. Other notables chosen that year in the first round included Bobby Holik, Olaf Kolzig and Bill Guerin, but Chyzowski could never handle the pace of the NHL.

After the baby-faced Sundin posed for pictures in his blue Nords' sweater, debate quickly began about his availability. His army service remained to be served, but no one saw that as a big hurdle. What did loom as a major headache was the contract with the parent club, Djurgarden. Not blind to Sundin's potential, Djurgarden officials had been plotting during the off-season and, before Perrone arrived on the scene, had browbeat Sundin into an undervalued four-year deal worth about $1,000 US a month.

It wasn't a problem so long as Sundin remained at home, but after his first year with Djurgarden and exposure to the national team, the piddly deal presented a legal snag to attend Quebec's 1990 training camp.

Sundin and Perrone attempted to wriggle away, but in a nasty and effective campaign, Djurgarden officials portrayed him as a traitor. Public opinion was anti-Sundin and the club even tried to turn teammates against him. They further turned up the heat by threatening to ban him from international hockey.

Sundin was mortified at what was happening, but eventually the Nords paid Djurgarden a six-figure sum to buy out the contract as well as any development fees.

The story had a rather comic ending, as Gauthier spirited Sundin out of Stockholm in disguise in the summer of 1990 to escape any last-minute court wrangling on the part of the Swedes.

"The people were hard on him," Nordstrom said. "But today, I think they realize he was only doing what he had to do for his career."

The 1989 draft was a strong one and included current NHL stars such as Bobby Holik, Olaf Kolzig and Bill Guerin.

4 The Nordiques

A 19-year-old Sundin spent his first days in Canada like reclusive Swedish film star Greta Garbo.

"He hid out in an apartment while the contract was being settled and didn't say a word for almost his first year," former teammate Craig Wolanin said with a laugh. "He wore the same sweatpants to the rink every day—with no socks."

On the ice, Sundin was anything but a wallflower. His regular-season debut was in the Hartford Civic Center, the backdrop for a couple of watershed events in Sundin's career. He scored a third-period goal against Peter Sidorkiewicz of the Whalers to cap a 3–3 rally.

Life with the young, dynamic Nordiques suited Sundin fine.

"It was an ideal place to start," Wolanin said. "The city had a European feel to it, there was a cast of equal age and the team was willing to take its time developing young talent."

Sundin, Joe Sakic, Owen Nolan and Ron Tugnutt would go on to be some of the most dominating NHLers of the 1990s. Sundin had a touch of homesickness, running up huge transatlantic phone bills, but enjoyed his spare time in the company of Wolanin, Curtis Leschyshyn and later Chris Simon.

"We weren't exactly the Brat Pack," Wolanin said. "It was more a case of four single guys who couldn't cook just hanging around together."

Chicago netminder Ed Belfour won the Calder Trophy in '90–'91, with rookie scoring leader Sergei Fedorov the runner-up. But Sundin's 23 goals were just eight fewer than Fedorov's, while he and Boston's Ken Hodge Jr. ended up with 59 points in a tie for second among rookies.

At first unsure of how he would adapt to the speed of the NHL and more than double the games of Nacka's schedule, the experience only whetted Sundin's appetite. He played all 80 games, an ironman trait that was to continue.

"Mats was a happy-go-lucky guy," Pierre Page recalled. But he also had to be toughened up.

Where the Nordiques went hungry was in the standings. The club compiled just 36 wins in Sundin's first two seasons and missed the playoffs three out of four times. Sundin himself was the legacy

Opposite: **Despite the culture shock of living in a foreign country, Sundin managed to score 24 goals in his first year and finished tied for second place in rookie scoring with 59 points.**

of a last-place finish when the Nords used their next first overall choice in 1991 on Eric Lindros. Sundin shared the excitement that gripped Quebec that spring with the thought of the fabulous Lindros joining the burgeoning stable of stars. But as the Lindros soap opera dragged on and the latter's disdain of the Nords' organization became clear, Sundin echoed the team's frustration and disappointment.

Sundin posted 17 more points in '91–'92, another losing season, but one that ended with the Lindros trade to the Flyers. Bolstered by Mike Ricci, Steve Duchesne and Ron Hextall and with Sundin and Sakic getting more than 100 points, the Nordiques scored 351 in '92–'93. Leading the way was Sundin, with 114 points and an astounding 30-game points streak of 21 goals and 25 assists, which still stands as the NHL's longest streak in the 1990s and has been bettered only by the retired Gretzky and Mario Lemieux.

Unfortunately, everyone's image of that long awaited playoff test for the Nords was of Page blasting a flustered-looking Sundin on the bench in the midst of the Nords blowing a 2–0 series lead to eventual Cup champion Montreal.

Both men still insist the incident was overblown, an argument about a missed coverage assignment on a key Habs' goal, and not, as many suggested, Page lambasting Sundin's quiet four-point effort in the series.

"What people don't understand is that that was the best season in the history of the club," Page said. "We wanted to win it all and we were trying to get every last ounce out of our young players—perhaps too quickly. And that's maybe where I made mistakes."

The cloud lingered into the next season, as the Nords took a step backwards on the ice. Sundin and others felt the wrath of Page again in the press, but there was the added weight of contract squabbles. The team awarded Sakic a new $2.8-million deal and Forsberg received similar riches before he even played an NHL game. But Sundin, in the third year on his first contract that paid him $900,000, did not have his deal readdressed as he said he'd been promised. He scored just 13 goals in the final 55 games of '93–'94.

"He was making news for all the wrong reasons and it weighed on him pretty good," Wolanin said. "Mats is not the kind of guy who is comfortable in that situation. What he wants to be known for is his ability to play hockey."

The natives were restless in Quebec as the club stumbled to a 76-point finish. One man sued the team for falsely advertising it was a contender. Another day, a group of fans met them at the airport after

Opposite: **Now both captains of their respective teams, Mats Sundin and Eric Lindros were almost teammates after the Nordiques drafted Lindros first overall in the 1991 draft. But Lindros refused to sign with Quebec and was eventually traded to the Philadelphia Flyers for several players including Sundin's fellow countryman, Peter Forsberg.**

a road loss and serenaded them with the Beatles' Yellow Submarine, changing the chorus to "We all cheer for a yellow hockey team...."

Rocket Richard, Guy Lafleur and former Habs' coach Jean Perron all lined up to take their shots at Coach Page and Nordiques' owner Marcel Aubut in the media. Page was eventually fired, and it was clear one of the young guns would have to be sacrificed for more veteran leadership. As he flew home, Sundin knew he would likely be the one to go.

But as he wandered the Torne Lappmark late that June, a rescue mission was underway hundreds of miles away in a Hartford hotel room.

Opposite: **Sundin continued to perform well as he grew more comfortable in Quebec. He steadily improved his game and scored 114 points in the 1992-93 season.**

Below: **Despite his past offensive glories, in 1993-94 Sundin suffered an off-year. After the Nordiques' poor playoff performance against the Montreal Canadiens, his days in Quebec were numbered.**

5 The Trade

The Leafs' war committee convened on the night before the 1994 draft with a lively debate.

For two straight years, the veteran-laden team had made it to the Conference final and had been turned back. The wild ride of '93 under new coach Pat Burns had come up one win short of making the finals, then Pat Quinn's hefty Vancouver lineup disposed of the Leafs fairly easily in '94. Like the Nords, the Leafs were at a crossroads.

"If we were going to stay in it, we needed a bold move to change our lineup," Fletcher said. "We couldn't do it through the draft, not when we sat at No. 22 in the order."

Toronto's need was obvious: a young, creative forward, preferably a second-line centre, to take the pressure off Gilmour. As they perused Quebec's roster, they could see it was loaded up front, but

In 1994-95, Pat Burns and the Maple Leafs' braintrust felt that Sundin was the missing piece the team needed to reach the NHL finals.

Sakic and Forsberg were untouchable and Nolan had an unfavorable reputation at the time. Fletcher and assistant GM Bill Watters, the Leafs' contract point man, ran their fingers down the Nords' roster and stopped at Sundin, but it was Nords' owner Marcel Aubut and new GM Pierre Lacroix who made the first overtures as Sundin's contract boondoggle increased.

Fletcher wasn't surprised when the rudderless Nordiques asked for his captain, Clark. Coming off a career-best 46 goals, Clark was one of Burns' top lieutenants, but worked quietly in relation to the high profile Burns and Gilmour.

Fletcher couldn't hope to land Sundin in a one-for-one for Clark, who was five years older, despite their shared status as former No. 1 picks. Pieces were quickly added to the deal, with Lacroix insisting on Leafs' reliable defenceman Sylvain Lefebvre and Leafs' prospect Landon Wilson. He also wanted the Leafs to pick up any outstanding development fees to Djurgarden.

Fletcher wanted speedy winger Todd Warriner, a former Nords' first-rounder, and defenceman Garth Butcher to offset Lefebvre's departure.

The Toronto Sun got wind of a Sundin deal on the night before the draft, and a late play by the Los Angeles Kings to get Lefebvre for the seventh pick in the draft almost derailed the Quebec talks. It wasn't until Fletcher, Lacroix and Aubut were walking into the Civic Center the next morning that the deal came together. Fletcher successfully held out for a switch in draft positions, in an ultimately failed attempt to grab Brett Lindros 10th overall.

The Leafs braced for the worst back home as the deal was announced.

"We'd talked about how negative the fans might react the night before," Stellick said. "It was a gutsy move by Cliff. Punch Imlach

Wendel Clark would return to the Toronto Maple Leafs twice after being one of the players traded to Quebec as part of the Sundin deal in 1994.

Left and following: Upon his arrival, Sundin had an immediate impact on the Maple Leafs, tallying an assist in his first game. Since 1994-95 he has been the team's scoring leader each year while also remaining an impressively durable player who misses few games due to injury.

Opposite: **Breakaway speed and a long reach make Sundin difficult for opposing players to contain.**

always said, 'he who gets the best player wins the trade,' and we received a very undervalued star in Mats. But we knew how much people cared for Wendel."

Public opinion was certainly against the trade, with Cherry leading the way. An emotional farewell press conference by Clark didn't help Fletcher's cause.

"We agonized over this," Fletcher said when the media mob cornered him in Hartford. "I love Wendel. But my job is to make this team better."

Fletcher's next words were prophetic.

"When Doug moves on in five years or whatever, Mats will only be 27. He'll be an impact player for years."

Burns acknowledged his new star had better develop a thick skin, but snapped, "I hope people don't expect Mats to go out and fight Bob Probert. That's not him."

Grief about Clark gave way to curiosity about Sundin, but not even the Leafs could find him for the first few days.

"We were about to send a Sherpa guide to find him," Stellick said with a laugh.

In Sweden there was much more positive press, including criticism of the Nords for mistreatment of Sundin and major disappointment that Sundin and Forsberg would not be able to play together the following year. Salming gave the deal a stamp of approval as well and predicted Sundin would one day make Toronto's impatient fans grateful for the deal.

As Sundin has matured, he has also gained size and strength through off-season weight training. Sundin's physical training has added an element of power to his game that allows him to drive hard to the net and break through opposing defenders.

How Swede it Is

The Leafs have been a leader in developing Swedish talent since the doors to Europe opened in the 1970s.

Borje Salming and Inge Hammarstrom were signed to play in the '73–'74 season. Sundin is a six-time member of the NHL all-star team. The Leafs also made Anders Hedberg their top scout and, later, assistant general manager. Thommie Bergman, the first Swedish import to play in the NHL, is now Toronto's European scout, and in Sundin the Leafs have the first European ever drafted first overall.

Previous: Always the focus of opposing teams' attentions, Sundin is surrounded by a group of Edmonton Oilers.

Above: Curtis Joseph fails to stop Sundin's drive to the net. As teammates with the Leafs, they form one of the most dominating twosomes in the NHL.

Opposite: Sundin celebrates after scoring on Jose Theodore of the Montreal Canadiens.

6 Life with the Leafs

Sundin walked into the Leafs' dressing room on the morning of February, 24, 1998, to an immediate roasting by teammates.

"Here he comes," crowed goaltender Glenn Healy, "the most eligible bachelor in Canada today."

"I hope you're buying us lunch—and dinner," shouted another.

Sundin smiled, a little red from embarrassment, but with plenty of green to compensate. He had just been at the Gardens' Hot Stove Lounge at a press conference announcing his new four-year $22.8-million US contract, making him the highest paid Leaf in club history. His annual $1.8-million salary was about to increase five-fold.

"I was talking with my Dad about the deal a few days before it was finalized and he's going 'Sign it! Sign it!'" Sundin said with a chuckle.

The deal, which Sundin and agent Mike Barnett agreed to as Mats jumped on a plane to the Nagano Olympics, was a huge relief to everyone in the Leafs' camp. New club president Ken Dryden honoured a promise from Fletcher to reopen Sundin's outdated contract, which had a year to run at about $2 million.

Sundin clearly liked the team and the city, but he craved the diamond Cup ring that countryman Forsberg now wore with pride. Before putting pen to paper, Sundin exacted a promise from Leafs' management that the Leafs would be moving to a new arena and would open the vault to start building a team that could make the playoffs.

Sundin's part of the bargain was to sign a long-term deal to avoid Group 2 free agency, as well as give the Leafs a chance at a new pact when Sundin is 30 and a year shy of total free agency.

Sundin is now among the world's top-paid entertainers, whose base salary for 2000–01 will peak at $7.5 million US. He's tied into the Leafs' lucrative team bonus plan for feats such as shutouts and has a string of profitable endorsements. Yet he's also worked at keeping a pledge he made that day at the Hot Stove—that the money wouldn't change him, on or off the ice.

"He's never talked down to people, even the youngest guys on our team," Domi said. "He's never been one to make a big speech, but when he does say something, people listen."

When rookie defenceman Tomas Kaberle became disheartened with an extended benching in the middle of '98–'99, Sundin was "like a father to him," said Kaberle's own dad, Frantisek. "Tomas was still a boy when he came to Toronto, and Mats made a difference."

Sundin monitors the team chemistry the Leafs had tried so hard to achieve for years and finally accomplished under Quinn. When the Leafs took a bus from Anaheim to Los Angeles after a win in the long and losing '97–'98 season, Sundin stopped at a video store and purchased three Simpsons' tapes so the fun and frivolity could continue on the highway. He makes sure the food, munchies and drinks are plentiful if the Leafs have extended treks and tries to organize off-day trips, such as visit to the White House during a

Tomas Kaberle is one of the most promising young defencemen in the league and a major reason why the Leafs emerged as Stanley Cup contenders in 1998-99 and 1999-2000.

Quinn and Sundin share a laugh during a practice session. When Pat Quinn was hired as Leafs coach he brought with him a strategy of speed and puck movement that led to the Leafs finishing the 1998-99 season as the highest scoring team in the NHL.

48-hour stop in Washington.

In the 1999 pre-season, when the training camp roster was an unwieldy 30-plus, he made sure there would be some team meals so the newcomers wouldn't feel slighted.

Sundin won't ever be Tiger Williams when it comes to colourful quotes, but he's gained respect in Toronto for his availability, even after the team's switch to larger quarters at the ACC made many Leafs less visible after games.

"Let's face it," Wolanin said. "When you're blond, Swedish, 6'4" and captain of the Leafs, you'll be noticed."

He doesn't mind the high-profile charity work expected of a Leafs' star, but keeps it manageable within the team's schedule.

"He doesn't make large gestures to specific charities, but a lot of the stuff he does, people will never see," said a team official. "He understands the big picture. He knows an extra 30 seconds with a disadvantaged kid can mean all the difference in the world."

Sundin has benefited greatly from his association with the Canadian-born Barnett and International Management Group (IMG). Barnett was one of four Canadians named to the Sporting News's 1999 Top 100 Most Powerful People In Sports. Barnett's IMG stable, headlined by Wayne Gretzky, Sundin, Jaromir Jagr and Sergei Fedorov, also includes new Swedish stars Daniel and Henrik Sedin.

Sundin and Gretzky would cross paths many times in the 1990s.

All of the Maple Leafs are active in the Toronto community, yet none are in higher demand with the fans both young and old, than the captain.

Following: **Sundin crashes into the St. Louis net during a game in March of 1999.**

Previous: Two Pittsburgh defencemen and the Penguins' goalie can only watch as Sundin, with a signature move, shoots the puck between the legs of Kevin Hatcher and straight into the net.

Left: An Ottawa defender tackles Sundin a moment too late as he flips the puck over the glove-hand of Senators' netminder Ron Tugnutt.

Above: Wayne Gretzky participated in the ceremonial faceoff between Sundin and Rangers captain Brian Leech in the game prior to the 1999 Hall of Fame induction ceremonies.

Below: Sundin and Tie Domi celebrate a Domi goal. The two are close friends on and off the ice.

Only these two and Mario Lemieux have had scoring streaks of 30 or more games in league history, with Sundin's run of 30 in '92–'93 holding up as the longest of the decade.

Gretzky and Sundin got to know each other well as Western Conference linemates in the 1997 All-Star game in Boston, one of five that Sundin has played in. (A Leaf record.) They filmed a McDonald's commercial where they pretended to one-up each other with trick shots that would ricochet off various parts of the Gardens, such as the scoreclock, before landing in the net.

In January 2000, Sundin led all centres on the world All-Star team with more than a half-million votes for the starting line-up at the 50th annual All-Star game being held in Toronto. Sundin has fueled hundreds of thousands of dollars in the sale of replica Leafs sweaters, with the once awkward but now widely accepted No. 13. Like Joseph and Domi, he is also prominent on T-shirts, posters and photos. After arriving in Toronto, Gord Stellick convinced Sundin to switch from his Jofa helmet to a North American model to help toughen-up his image. He was one of Nike's biggest head-to-toe endorsers, but signed a multi-year, six-figure equipment deal in 1999 with CCM.

A fair golfer who often plays with team enforcer Domi, Sundin will often flip the channel in the dressing room or hotel to tournaments involving countryman Jesper Parnavik. He listens to the hip-hop band A Tribe Called Quest, declares Jack Nicholson as his favourite actor and the dark comedy *Fargo* his top movie.

Sundin still lists his favourite pro sports team as the flashy and often arrogant Dallas Cowboys, even though he is their alter ego. Though he could afford a farm in the country such as the one teammate Curtis Joseph has, he and girlfriend Tina Fagerstrom live in the downtown Toronto high-rise where Sundin has resided in relative anonymity for a few years. Sundin's favourite car is an Audi S8, but he can walk the few blocks to the Air Canada Centre if he chooses.

"More and more fans come up to me on the street, but it's not a (threatening presence)," he said during '98–'99 when club fortunes

In 1998, the Leafs signed superstar, free-agent goaltender Curtis Joseph. A huge factor in the team's resurgence, he and Sundin will compete against each other in the 2000 All-Star game in Toronto.

soared and long suffering supporters seemed to be everywhere. "They're good people, just hockey fans, and they want to show you their appreciation for what we've done. I get flowers all the time and cards that say 'keep up the good work.'"

Sundin is a bit more extravagant with his lifestyle in Sweden, where he has supervised construction of a summer house in Norrtelje, about 45 minutes north of Stockholm, an exclusive seaside town on the Baltic.

Though attention in North America is more fixed on his job at the rink, Sundin's love life is a closely followed story back home. Ballet dancer Anna Hansen was a long-time companion who spent a year in Quebec with him, while a few years ago, he had a casual friendship with Anki Edvinsson, a leggy, blonde meteorologist on Stockholm TV. A

Previous: **Leaf fans hope that together Sundin and Joseph will lead the team to their first Stanley Cup victory since 1967.**

Right: **Mats Sundin and girlfriend Tina Fagerstrom.**

Opposite: **Always at the centre of things, Sundin is mobbed by teammates during the 1999 playoffs.**

Following: **A pair of Dallas defenders cross their sticks in an effort to impede Sundin's progress towards the net. The Stars would go on to win the Stanley Cup in 1999.**

photo with Finnish violin soloist Linda Lampenius during the world championships in 1998 also had tongues wagging, but Sundin was spoken for.

It was big news when the pretty, red-haired Tina was first seen with him at the '99 all-star game in Tampa, but she has spent their two-year relationship maintaining a separate career working with the mentally challenged at a facility in Stockholm and may pursue a similar path in Toronto.

The couple has not announced wedding plans, but Sundin joked with Swedish reporters during the summer that his swinger days were coming to an end.

"I'm more mature," he told *Expressen*. "I've quit running out at nights….I'm through with that part of my life."

7 Quest for the Cup

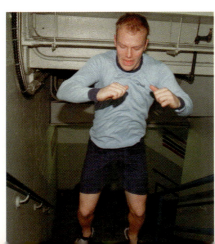

The first time Sundin swung a stick in anger after losing the Buffalo series was at a golf outing at Devil's Pulpit near Toronto. Domi watched in awe as Sundin clobbered his tee shots.

"You could tell he was on a mission for the coming season," Domi said. "From that first day back from Sweden, just by the sound of his voice, you could tell he was more serious than ever."

He looked strikingly different, too. Phil Walker, the Leafs' strength and conditioning coach, took one look at Sundin's chiseled face and knew he'd followed a good weight training program. When the Leafs scored a higher average in Walker's camp fitness tests, Sundin's VO2 numbers, which measure the body's ability to use oxygen, were greatly improved.

For the first time in years, the Leafs weren't just using camp as a conduit to the first week of games in October. They were already steeling themselves for the playoffs months down the road. Before Christmas, they were already at 50 points, halfway to a club record 100.

Changes around Sundin were swift and dramatic. The handful of players Quinn decided were weak links the previous spring were traded. In came bigger defencemen such as Cory Cross and younger, more tenacious checkers such as Kevyn Adams.

Sundin needed no alarm clock to wake him for the 1999-2000 season. He was pumped after getting halted seven wins from a

Stanley Cup and finally experiencing the wild ride of the playoffs, with high tempo hockey every second night and a city gone bonkers.

"It made me hungry," he said. "I want to go all the way."

Sundin had put together an 83-point season in '98–'99, then added 16 in 17 playoff games, the only Leaf to play in all 99 combined contests. Free to roam the ice more by Quinn and backed by Joseph, strong second-line centres and a compatible right winger in free agent Steve Thomas, Sundin finished 11th in NHL scoring.

The Leafs had to take out extra space in their post-season media guide to list their deeds, which included leading the league in goals for the first time in decades, a club record 45 wins, a 37–1–2 record when ahead after 40 minutes and the best overtime mark of

Above: **Curtis Joseph kicks a puck away as Sundin cruises through the crease.**

Opposite top: **Mats hugs linemate Steve Thomas who had one of the best years of his career while playing on Sundin's line in 1998-1999.**

Opposite bottom: **Sundin has dedicated himself to a rigorous off-season training program.**

Many teams try to wear-down the Leafs' captain physically by checking him heavily throughout the game. The Philadelphia Flyers employed this tactic without success in the 1999 playoffs.

6–1–7. Sundin went to the All-Star game and nearly upstaged Gretzky with a four-point performance and earned an assist when Thomas won the first game over Montreal at the ACC in overtime.

"I feel it's very important to (establish myself)," he said on the eve of the '99 post-season. "I've played in a lot of world championships and other tournaments, but this is what playing in the NHL is all about."

The Maple Leafs beat the Pittsburgh Penguins in six games to advance to the conference finals in 1999.

He entered the opening playoff series against the Philadelphia Flyers without having ever survived a first round as a Leaf or Nordique. The Flyers' trap snared Sundin and a few high-flying mates in the early going. The line of Marc Bureau, Keith Jones and Jody Hull was particularly effective.

But Quinn had already asked his captain to be a presence everywhere on the ice and the wins would take care of themselves.

"He may not be a major scoring factor for us in the playoffs," Quinn predicted at a mini-camp in Barrie. "What we want him to do is to be reliable in his own end.

"I don't care if he's the ultimate thing that this team revolves around. Even if he doesn't score, he has the capability of giving us that confidence that things are going well in a game."

The Leafs wound up winning the series with just nine goals, breaking a 50-year club record for lowest output in a six-game playoff series.

Czech superstar Jaromir Jagr checks Sundin closely.

The Pittsburgh Penguins were a tough nut to crack as well. While Eric Lindros had missed the Flyers' series, Sundin had to contend with Jaromir Jagr, a duel that dated back to the 1990 world junior hockey championships. After a loss in the series' opener, Sundin found himself watched from coast to coast with the Leafs becoming the lone Canadian team in Cup contention. But he shoved four points down his critics' throats in a 4–2 Game 2 win.

"He must have ice in his veins," winger Garry Valk observed of Sundin's refusal to snap.

At the end of the Pittsburgh series, Sundin had three goals and four assists with six points at even strength. Jagr had four even-strength points head-to-head against Sundin, whose line worked well in tandem with mauling Russian defencemen Danny Markov and Dmitry Yushkevich. Sundin was a plus-five in the series and plus-five in Toronto's four wins. Jagr was a minus-two in the series, a difference of seven even-strength goals.

Sundin didn't waver as the Leafs went into the conference final against Buffalo, but Thomas couldn't hide a debilitating shoulder injury, and no one could play an effective left wing on the line. Ninety minutes shy of June 1, the Leafs ran out of gas.

"I got more experience in these 17 games than in my previous years in the league," Sundin said amid the disappointment. "Everything came together. The years you miss the playoffs, you look at the guys who play two or three rounds and you wonder how they do it.

"Once you get there yourself, you just find yourself with so much energy you never know you had."

But the word was that Quinn had verbally needled his captain to

To make it to the Stanley Cup Finals in 2000 the Leafs will first have to get past hard working, physical teams like Buffalo and Philadelphia.

go one better in their last face-to-face meeting after the Sabres' series. Sundin played their talk down and Quinn wouldn't discuss it, but there was no mistaking the two were on the same page when the '99–'00 camp convened in Barrie.

What seemed like an impossible log-jam ahead of them when the Leafs moved east seemed to be affording them a chance to move up. New Jersey and Philadelphia, the biggest teams in terms of size, have proven to have Achilles heels in playoffs with scoring and goal-tending problems respectively. Clubs such as Pittsburgh, Buffalo, Boston, Florida and Carolina can only beat Toronto's talented roster by outworking it.

Sundin had further reason to feel optimistic because the league was supposed to do an about-face on the crease rule, giving big centres such as himself more leeway in the blue paint to utilize their reach and their body mass.

Sundin tore out of the gate with a goal in each of his first three games before misfortune struck.

Following: A trio of Penguins can only watch as Sundin shovels the puck past Pittsburgh goalie Tom Barasso.

The Calgary goaltender sprawls helplessly as Sundin demonstrates that he does indeed possess one of the NHL's best backhands.

Sundin recovered incredibly quickly after fracturing his ankle early in the 1999-2000 season

A couple of days after a false radio report had him hospitalized with a broken leg, Sundin truly was cursed when he took a Radek Bonk drive off his right ankle in a game in Ottawa. Though he finished the contest, his ankle was badly swollen the next day. X-rays showed a non-displaced fracture, and a five- to six-week recovery was predicted.

Sundin began an aggressive therapy program immediately, aided enormously by the conditioning work he'd undertaken in the summer. Every day was a monotonous four-hour rotation of an ultrasound machine, cold tub, compression bags and acupuncture.

"By the end of the day, you are more tired than when you're playing," Sundin observed.

But the recuperation wound up lasting just nine games. The medical marvel was back before four weeks had elapsed, and he was challenging for the team lead in points again with his new Swedish left winger, Jonas Hoglund.

Quinn has tried various ways of expanding Sundin's role outside of the obvious double shifting to bring Sundin close to the

27 to 30 minutes a game he's capable of playing. Quinn's used him as the point man on the power play in hopes of utilizing his hard shot and at least considered him as a winger, figuring he'd scare the wits out of checkers as he cut through open ice at full steam. Sundin had once played with Gilmour at centre and Clark on the left side.

It was 17 months following the Quebec trade that Sundin and Clark finally faced each other, Oct. 10, 1995. Both men said all the right things leading up to the game, but the Gardens crowd unwittingly stoked Sundin by giving Clark a rousing ovation in his pre-game skate, outstripping Sundin's official introduction during home opener ceremonies. But it was Sundin who scored at 8:02 of the first period, underlining the changing of the guard by smashing his fist into the back glass in a rare display of emotion.

Mats celebrates after scoring against the New York Islanders and former Leaf captain Wendel Clark in 1995.

"I was letting off some steam I guess," Sundin said later. "He deserved the cheers, but at the same time, it helped us out." Clark would return twice to the Leafs, once in a 1996 trade and again as a free agent in 2000.

Sundin had a positive relationship with Gilmour as well and wound up assisting on the latter's 1,000th NHL point, about a year before Gilmour's trade effectively left the leadership mantle to No. 13.

Sundin might fancy retiring with the Leafs' 'C', since the six men who wore it since George Armstrong hoisted the '67 Cup did not finish their careers in Toronto. Sundin will be able to pass along the same advice Sittler has given Clark, Gilmour and himself.

"It's one of the greatest jobs in Canada," Sittler said one night as he was watching Sundin cavort at the ACC. "Mats may not realize it until he retires, but look at the longevity of those who went before us: Dave Keon, Syl Apps, Ted Kennedy and George Armstrong.

"If you play well as captain of the Toronto Maple Leafs, people will remember you forever."

Using his back hand, Sundin protects the puck while circling behind the Islanders' net.

Kevin Hatcher of the New York Rangers hooks Sundin as he tries to shoot.

Following: Sundin and Joseph model the jerseys that the World and North American teams will wear at the 2000 All-Star game in Toronto. Sundin is the leading vote getter for the World Team and he and Maple Leafs defenceman, Dimitri Yuskevitch will play against the North American team and Joseph, the starting goalie for the game.

Stats

Year	Team	GP	G	A	Pts	+/-	PIM	S	S%	PPG
1999-00	Toronto Maple Leafs	38	21	19	40	2	14	82	25.6	1.05

Trophies

1999-00	Played in NHL All-Star Game
1998-99	Played in NHL All-Star Game
1997-98	Played in NHL All-Star Game
1995-96	Played in NHL All-Star Game
1993-94	Swedish–World All-Star Team
1991-92	Swedish–World All-Star Team
1990-91	Swedish–World All-Star Team

Trades

6/28/1994
Toronto Maple Leafs traded Wendel Clark, Sylvain Lefebvre, Landon Wilson and 1st round selection (Jeffrey Kealty) in 1994 to the Quebec Nordiques for Mats Sundin, Garth Butcher, Todd Warriner and 1st round selection (previously acquired from the Philadelphia Flyers, later traded to the Washington Capitals – Nolan Baumgartner) in 1994.

6/17/1989
Drafted by the Quebec Nordiques in the 1st round (1st overall) in 1989.

Career Stats

Year	Team	Lea	GP	G	A	Pts	+/-	PIM	S	S%	PPG
1998-99	Toronto Maple Leafs	NHL	82	31	52	83	22	58	209	14.8	1.01
1997-98	Toronto Maple Leafs	NHL	82	33	41	74	-3	49	219	15.1	0.90
1997-98	Olympic Team	Swe	4	3	0	3	-	4	-	-	0.75
1996-97	Toronto Maple Leafs	NHL	82	41	53	94	6	59	281	14.6	1.15
1995-96	Toronto Maple Leafs	NHL	76	33	50	83	8	46	301	11.0	1.09
1994-95	Toronto Maple Leafs	NHL	47	23	24	47	-5	14	173	13.3	1.00
1994-95	Djurgarden	Swe	12	7	2	9	-	14	-	-	0.75
1993-94	Quebec	NHL	84	32	53	85	1	60	226	14.2	1.01
1992-93	Quebec	NHL	80	47	67	114	21	96	215	21.9	1.43
1991-92	Quebec	NHL	80	33	43	76	-19	103	231	14.3	0.95
1990-91	Quebec	NHL	80	23	36	59	-24	58	155	14.8	0.74
1989-90	Djurgarden	Swe	34	10	8	18	-	16	-	-	0.53
1988-89	Nacka	Swe	25	10	8	18	-	18	-	-	0.72
-	Career	NHL	731	317	438	755	9	557	2092	15.2	1.03
-	Career	Swe	46	17	10	27	-	30	-	-	0.59